I Choose to L.I.V.E.

"Embracing the Real Me"

SAUNYA M. WILLIAMS, PH.D.

3G Publishing, Inc.
Loganville, Ga 30052
www.3gpublishinginc.com
Phone: 1-888-442-9637

©2015 Saunya M. Williams, Ph.D., LLC. All rights reserved.

No part of this book may be reproduced or transmitted in any form or by any means, electronic or mechanical, including photocopying, recording, or by any information storage and retrieval system, without the written permission of the author.

First published by 3G Publishing, Inc. (November)(2015)

ISBN: 978-1-941247-17-4

All scripture quotations are taken from the New King James Version (NKJV) of the Bible.

Photography done by Neville Simpson

Printed in the United States of America

Because of the dynamic nature of the Internet, any web addresses or links contained in this book may have changed since publication and may no longer be valid. The views expressed in this work are solely those of the author and do not necessarily reflect the views of the publisher, and the publisher hereby disclaims any responsibility for them.

To my mommy, Linda Harris, you encouraged me to share my story without reservation. This book exists because of your unselfish support…thank you!

I love you forever plus one day!

- Saun

Table of Contents

INTRODUCTION	7
CHAPTER 1	11
LOVE	
Outside-In Type	11
Material Possession	12
Professional Achievement	14
Social Status	15
Aesthetic Appeal	16
Inside-Out Type	19
Internal Presence of God	19
Front-Row Seat	21
CHAPTER 2	25
INVEST	
Garbage	25
Plastic Bag	28
No Progress	30
Goals	32
Planned Purpose	32
God's Blueprint	35
CHAPTER 3	39
VICTORY	
Divine GPS	39
Victim to Victor	42
CHAPTER 4	47
ENCOURAGE	
Mirror Reflection	47
Duplicate Your Present	47

Recall Your Past   49
Two-Dimensional Network   51

CONCLUSION   55

L.I.V.E. SUMMARY SCRIPTURES   57

ABOUT THE AUTHOR   59

NOTES   61

INTRODUCTION

One year in particular, I traveled for approximately 40 out of 52 weeks and spent over 150 nights in various hotels. The extensive travel was required for my job so I was accustomed to "life on the road," as I considered my lifestyle. After experiencing so many challenges, I was certain that I had put the worst of them behind me. Unexpectedly, the weight of being molested as a child had started to resurface, and the weight soon became an unbearable encumbrance. The fact that the burden was so heavy was an indication that my previous attempts to bury that particular burden had not been as successful as I thought.

For many years, I had been living with a forward-thinking motto and more self-confidence so I was surprised to realize that my struggle with being molested was very much alive. I was revisiting the most traumatic battle of my life, and my feeling of being a conqueror had suddenly vanished. My chest felt like a building had collapsed upon me, and I doubted that I was strong enough to overcome the same battle again. I turned to God for understanding and asked, "Why me and why now?"

Simultaneously, I had been in a long-distance relationship with Raider for almost five years so I welcomed the opportunity to minimize the distance between us. I thought that my travel schedule would benefit our relationship by affording us with more time together. Quickly, I discovered that the excitement that he had shown toward me was not sincere. I was well aware that Raider had been experiencing financial hardship over the years, but I never imagined the enormous depth of his deception. I could not comprehend why Raider preferred to continuously live in a path of self-destruction, which included lies, theft, and domestic abuse.

Until then, I never realized that I had created an exhausting role for myself by relying on my personal relationships to fill such a huge void. I had spent the majority of my life believing that a successful relationship with a man was my only way to experience real love. When I lost the very thing that I had believed was the key to my healing, I did not know what to do. My emotional capacity had been depleted, and I was no longer able to substitute the emptiness. The increase in amount of time that I had begun to spend alone caused me to question my beliefs. I said to God, "Now this too, but why?" and never heard an answer.

The combination of the resurrected shame of being molested and heartache from my failed relationship was such an emotional disaster for me. I would think about all that I had overcome and all that I had achieved up to that point, but my thoughts and feelings kept leading me toward defeat. Thus, the question, "Why me?" became the primary focus of my life at that time. My mind became inundated with thoughts of failure, and I could not make sense of the situation.

I was the leader of the mime ministry at my church, but I had lost both my faith and my praise. Shamefully, I did not know how to tell the other members of my ministry that I had given up on God and did not want to mime anymore. I had stopped believing in the Word of God and had no desire to worship Him at all. I did not feel comfortable with ministering the gospel that I had decided was false. As a result, I would find reasons to cancel our rehearsals and would delay our schedule to minister at church. I was convinced that God had completely abandoned me and that His presence was no longer in my life.

Each week, I would sit alone drowning in depression in my hotel room. The mere thought of food made me sick so my diet consisted of sleeping pills and wine, with occasional coffee or tea at work. Everything in me, on me, and about me was hurting so I just wanted to be numb or sleep. I never consciously attempted or planned to end my own life, but I would often think, "What if I do not wake up tomorrow morning and this is the last time that I close my eyes?" Honestly, I would not ponder that thought very long because I wanted to consume my sleeping pill and wine as soon as possible. I was in such a rush to not feel any pain that allowing my mind to contemplate anything else would have been too much time being wasted. Beyond that, I also did not consider the price of my addiction because my immediate relief was far more important to me at that time. Ultimately, my emotional paralysis became my place of refuge and comfort instead of God.

After several months, I had done so much to become detached from the world and God that I did not even recognize myself in the mirror. One morning in my hotel, I clearly heard, "Saunya, you are going to die, if you do not pull yourself together." The words were very simple, yet the delivery was so profound that I could ignore neither the message nor the messenger. Despite my blatant rejection and dismissal of God, I heard His voice loud and clear on that morning.

I responded back to God with a voice of triumph and declared that it was time for me to live again! At that moment, I began to think about what it meant for me to really live and realign myself with God. I went to the Merriam-Webster Dictionary for the definition of live, but I did not consider the various definitions to be sufficient fuel for my journey. As a result, I created the *L.I.V.E. Commitment*, which I defined as the following:

- I will LOVE myself

- I will INVEST in myself

- I will find VICTORY in myself

- I will ENCOURAGE myself

The *L.I.V.E. Commitment* quickly became the foundation for my healing and motivated me to remove the mask that I had worn for over two decades. Previously, I had believed that my testimony should be permanently hidden within the walls of my proverbial closet because I feared that exposing my truth would only lead to judgment by others. On the contrary, the exposure granted me with a liberty, and a reward that I could have never imagined. I was finally free from the shame of being molested as a child. I was able to feel guiltless and to be transparent for the first time in my life. Through the *L.I.V.E. Commitment*, God brought me out of the darkness that had been my place of solace for so many years. The real me was revealed, and a whole new world was before me.

Chapter 1

LOVE

Love can be expressed by using verbal as well as non-verbal communication. Some people express genuine and unselfish love toward others with ease. Some people depend on the love of others as a sense of security and validation. Love is a powerful force of emotion and stimulates people to act in a variety of ways. Unfortunately, I believe that love is too often misinterpreted, misused, and misplaced. In addition, I recognize that many people are in bondage, but they do not realize the existence of their personal chains. An external force is not always the culprit of bondage, but bondage can also be self-inflicted. In either case, bondage can influence how you determine your personal value and affect how you love yourself. I ask, "Do you love yourself 'outside-in' or 'inside-out'"?

Outside-In Type

I describe the "outside-in" type as a person who concentrates on presenting an appearance that is highly commended by others in an effort to conceal an internal struggle. In simple words, this type of person relies on external success to eliminate internal mess. I have discovered that this type of person does not possess humility as a strong suit while trying to deny an internal struggle. I am talking about an internal struggle like, but not limited to, bitterness, shame, insecurity, self-esteem or unforgiveness. I believe that misguided blame can also lead to a person not realizing the existence of an internal struggle. For example, some people will look away from themselves rather than toward themselves for the source of their problem.

The outside-in type tries to create an environment that enables their rewards of the external world to dominate their internal struggle. The goal is to empower external success so much that the internal struggle becomes dormant or seemingly non-existent all together. Unfortunately, this type of person has failed to recognize that it is impossible to conquer anything that he or she is not willing to confront. In the end, the outside-in type of person uses external success to create a facade that everyone else has come to believe is unpretentious.

Furthermore, the outside-in type of person is also more susceptible to being controlled by bondage. This person can become so engulfed in maintaining a fabricated character that their bondage may not be realized. To accompany this type, I have classified the following four categories of bondage: Material Possession, Professional Achievement, Social Status, and Aesthetic Appeal.

These four categories are not innately harmful, but these categories are often manipulated in a way that leads to an unhealthy relationship. Typically, bondage does not operate alone and partners up with a type of mask or camouflage. In this setting, I define bondage as what holds a person captive and camouflage as how that person dwells in that particular captivity. The outside-in type of person is a camouflage champion and focuses on concealing or altering the truth.

Material Possession

I define the bondage of Material Possession as when a person allows their personal value to be held hostage to the tangible property that they have acquired. I am referring to tangible items like clothing, houses, vehicles, and other things that are obtained to accommodate a person's desires. I am also talking about the material items that even cause some people to live beyond their financial resources. Some people are simply inspired by the material possessions that are popular in current culture, and some people are enamored by brand name.

When looking at an item, the item is often qualified and categorized by the reputation of its brand name. For example, certain brands are classified as having high quality and financial esteem while some brands are classified as having inferior quality and less incentive. The brand name is commonly used to make a statement about class and prestige. Personally, I agree that the brand name has the ability to make a particular item more or less attractive to a consumer. I also recognize that presumptions, whether positive or negative, are often made about an item based upon its brand.

Many of us are guilty of assessing other people or even ourselves with criteria that is similar to how we assess a brand. Do you feel that you are more qualified because of the brand of your material possessions? I have discovered that a lot of people will have a highly decorated exterior, but they have an extremely deteriorated interior. In addition, I believe that a lot of people spend too much time trying to imitate a brand instead of creating their own brand.

By creating your own brand, I am not suggesting that you should ever be for sale. I am referring to how you utilize your genuine characteristics and gifts to represent yourself. What are you using to build your personal brand? You cannot allow your personal brand to be dependent on external factors or material possessions because such things can change. Whether you are sitting on the curb of a street or flying 30,000 feet above ground in your private jet, your personal brand should remain the same.

Not long ago, I met a man that intentionally stated his residential zip code as a part of his introduction to ensure that I knew his financial status. During my first conversation with that man, he chose to boast about what he owned, where he vacationed, and how much spending money he would give me. I developed the impression that he was a bit self-absorbed because he talked as if the mere square footage of his home was his personal brand. I began to think that the direction of that man's worship was toward his material possessions, or better yet, himself. When I mentioned that I was in a complicated relationship, he said, "You two need to figure it out because

I'm trying to piss on my territory." Subsequently, I decided that my first conversation with that man would indeed be my last conversation with him.

Do you own your possessions or do your possessions own you? Do you have a particular possession that you love and worship more than God? We all have needs and wishes for a variety of material possessions, but we still have to be careful with prioritizing our possessions. With that being said, I do believe that an individual can have all sorts of material possessions without being bound to any of them. Regardless of the cost of your material possessions, I do not believe that you should ever pay the price with your soul. Since it is God who sustains you every day, it must be God who gets your worship.

Professional Achievement

I define the bondage of Professional Achievement as when a person allows their personal value to be held hostage to variables such as title, salary, or academic degree. While all of these attributes are wonderful to have, some people have attached a superiority complex to their professional success. After investing a lot of work and experiencing great success, many people become self-consumed and pour heavily into their own ego. Similarly, it is very easy to look at a person's resume and attempt to draw a simple conclusion, but a person's story cannot be written like a linear equation.

For instance, a person may be rich in reference to salary, but that person may be poor in reference to being saved. A person may have a name with an executive title, but that person's name may not be written in the Lamb's Book of Life. A person may be committed to exceling in the top percentile of higher education, but that person may have failed "101" of God's curriculum. At times, you may only see the effort that you have put forth, and the sacrifices that you have made along the way so you may feel that you deserve all of the credit. On the contrary, you must give all of the glory to God because there is no achievement that exceeds the favor that comes from Him.

Social Status

I define the bondage of Social Status as when a person allows their personal value to be held hostage to societal standards and praise. The praise from others is what some people use to appease their feelings of insecurity and inadequacy. I have witnessed how far some people will go to falsify details about themselves in an attempt to be more attractive and obtain more applause. With the advent of certain applications, there are people that depend on their number of "friends" or "followers" to stimulate self-esteem. The convenience of technology has given way for people to use social media, and the amount of "likes" that are received to try to boost their own prominence. Furthermore, several people seem to enjoy living their lives through the channels of social media and welcome the intrusive nature in an effort to gain attention.

Personally, I am a fan of social media because it provides an opportunity to reach those that would normally be unreachable and to communicate with the entire world. The popularity and technological evolution of social media has enabled pervasive use within our local and global societies. Equally, I also recognize that the use of social media can be harmful when malice is the intent. That is why I believe that we should all be cautious and particular about whom we call friend. Indeed, there is a difference between an acquaintance and a friend. How do you determine who gets added to the contact list of your social network? Are you motivated by the people that just know your name or by the people that actually seek to know you personally?

The good news is that God could not care less about your social status because His love is truly unconditional. God should never be treated like an acquaintance, and the communication that you have with Him should extend far beyond a casual post to His "spiritual page." You have to be intentional about having a personal relationship with God. When it comes to your connection with God, it is not about just knowing His name, but you must know God for yourself.

Aesthetic Appeal

I define the bondage of Aesthetic Appeal as when a person allows their personal value to be held hostage to their sense of beauty. I recognize that the classification of beauty can be rather subjective because what is beautiful to one person may not be beautiful to another. With this type of bondage, I am referring to how an individual identifies with beauty, and what makes that individual feel attractive. For example, some people may allow the social definitions and criteria to dictate what is beautiful while other people may establish their own measures. The emphasis of attractiveness is most often on the outward appearance so it is easy for a person to become heavily focused on personal aesthetics.

Out of all of the bondage categories that I described, I was bound to Aesthetic Appeal. From the age of 10-15, I was constantly molested, and physically and verbally abused by my stepfather. I was initially attracted to the attention because my stepfather was spending so much time with me, and I was the only child at 10 years of age. I enjoyed having a friend that was always available, but I soon realized that his attention was not of a friendly nature. My relationship with my stepfather would vacillate between him being my best friend and him being someone that I desperately tried to avoid.

When the abuse became more frequent, I did not know how to manage the emotional roller coaster that I was riding on because it never came to a stop. Subsequently, I was covered in emotional scars so I searched for a camouflage to provide aesthetic restoration. I connected beauty to love, which were the most important things that I felt had escaped me at a young age. I began to believe that my beauty was the key to genuine love, and that genuine love would accompany my beauty. As a result, I began to use my mother's cosmetics to try to cover my emotional wounds and appear to be someone that I was not.

As a young girl, all I could do was try to look beautiful and present myself as normal because I did not feel normal at all. In fact, I felt damaged, contaminated, and utterly destroyed because I was left alone to deal with the battle of being abused. I excelled academically, yet my stepfather told me that I was stupid and would never amount to anything. I was a virgin, yet he called me a whore. I was a child, yet he wanted me to perform the sexual acts of an adult. I was defenseless, yet he kept putting me in situations that required me to fight. I was innocent, yet he caused me to feel like I was sentenced to a lifetime of guilt.

I despised the things that my stepfather used to say to me, and the fact that I would feel like I was clothed in dirt. Being a child, I could not comprehend why I was being targeted and could not imagine what I had done to deserve such disgusting and inexcusable treatment. My cry seemed to always fall upon deaf ears, and my grasp for help seemed to always return void. Although my mind was twisted and confused, I was certain that I never wanted other people to develop a similar perception or to echo similar statements about me. I felt confident that wearing a mask was my only way to survive in a life that was such a horrible reality. From that point forward, I knew that makeup would be my solution and allow me to bandage the emotional poverty that had me bound.

Starting at the age of 11, I began to believe that I was worthless so makeup easily became my means to disguise my pain and enabled me to sketch a beautiful life onto an empty soul. I would sneak and use my mother's makeup to do the best that I could to make myself look pretty because I believed that the abuse had made me so ugly. I had learned about makeup by watching my mother so I was confident that I had enough skill to emulate her. I remember how I used to get chastised by my mother for always lying about wearing makeup. I would wipe off my makeup before I arrived home from school, but I did not realize that my red-stained lips and "raccoon eyes" were the keys to my guiltiness.

During those years, I always wished that I had a lock on my bedroom door to keep my stepfather from just walking in on me. On many occasions, I had to cover myself with only my two hands because he would time his uninvited entrance to catch me naked. My stepfather would also enter unannounced to expose his nude body to me. He would often position himself on top of me or next to me to try to initiate some level of intimacy between us. My stepfather was also adamant about kissing and would hold my face to prevent me from turning away. Beyond that, he would feel, grab, squeeze, and force his "impression" upon me at any time.

My stepfather would physically restrain me to keep me from moving and hit me for no reason. Frequently, he would slap me because I was not a willing participant of his sexual advances toward me. We never had sexual intercourse, but my stepfather always expressed his desires to me and asked me to pursue him for sex whenever I was ready. I truly believed that his confidence and aggression were greatly amplified by my mother's lack of attention to the abuse. I can vividly recall the times when my stepfather would molest me in the presence of my mother so that he could justify saying, "She does not care about you, and she does not care about what I do to you." Since my mother never said anything to him, I was abused for years.

My stepfather did not address me by my first name, but addressed me as "spoiled whore" or "spoiled bitch" during those years. My mother worked extensive hours and left me home alone with my stepfather, which was like the ultimate playground for him and complete misery for me. At one point, my mother even believed that he and I had bonded to form a relationship that was against her. I was under my stepfather's influence and would often play as his advocate, if it meant that he would leave me alone.

By the age of 12, I had become very active in things like concerts, roller skating, movies, dancing, and sleepovers at my friend's house. The more I tried to be active outside of the home, the more my stepfather would tell my mother a lie to make me stay at home. He would communicate false stories to ensure that I was not allowed to attend certain events or was completely restricted to remain at home. As a result, the amount of abuse from my stepfather increased and so did my rejection of him. In the end, I had become a physical and verbal warrior, but was an emotional catastrophe.

Once I graduated from college the first time, I upgraded my makeup from cheap to high-end and considered myself to be "runway-show" ready. I was convinced that my emotional scars and emptiness would never be discovered by anyone. Even though I knew that I was really broken, I was extremely determined to appear as whole so I continued to wear makeup as my camouflage. I desperately tried to see beauty in myself, but I could not see beyond the disdain that I had for myself.

To ensure that no one saw the unhappy person that I saw, my mask was my way of creating a visual that everyone could love. I was confident in my theory that beauty would lead to love. Thus, I thought that if I worked on my aesthetics hard enough, then I would eventually be able to love myself as a whole. I also believed that I had to be loved and to be saved by someone else before I could ever be happy with the real me. As a result, I spent many years in search of love and trying to end the hurting echoes of my soul.

Inside-Out Type

I describe the "inside-out" type as a person who focuses on maintaining an internal presence that does not waver in order to combat the vicissitudes of life. The impact of external change can be significant, which is why having internal stability is so important. Even when the world around you seems to be fragmented, the source of peace that is within you will prevail. Unfortunately, the "storms of life" are not included in the weather forecast so a fair warning is not possible by television, social media, or cellular phone. Life will undoubtedly present uncertainties that are designed to test a person's faith. Fortunately, the inside-out type of person understands that their strength is not self-generated because their strength is connected to a much greater power.

Internal Presence of God

The ferocity of a storm or weight of a burden can scare you into believing that a conqueror does not reside in you. At times, you may feel like resigning and surrendering to the enemy is your only option. While knowing that things in your external realm will encounter a variety of changes, you must rely on the internal presence of God to overcome the chaos. God is the ultimate problem solver and extends His services for free. Regardless of our individual merit, God is eternally gracious and merciful to all of us. The definition of mercy can be simply stated as not receiving the punishment that you do deserve, and the definition of grace can be simply stated as receiving the compassion that you do not deserve.

> "⁸ For by grace you have been saved through faith, and that not of yourselves; *it is* the gift of God, ⁹ not of works, lest anyone should boast." (Ephesians 2:8-9, NKJV)

> "¹ Oh, give thanks to the Lord, for *He is* good! For His mercy *endures* forever." (Psalm 136:1, NKJV)

Unfortunately, I spent many years without really knowing the presence of God in my life. The abuse that I suffered as a child had caused me to feel like I was polluted and without any value. Eventually, I accepted that even the colorful world of high-end makeup was not going to provide me with a permanent camouflage nor deliver me from my bondage. I had to realize that my personal supply was insufficient because God was the true sustenance for a healthy life. In essence, I began to rely on God's power to work through me and for me. I was triumphant because He also turned my fear of failure into fortitude. By recognizing the internal presence of God, I knew that I was well equipped for my journey and did not need to worry about the potential pitfalls that may have been ahead of me

Despite the unfortunate circumstances that you may experience, it is the internal presence of God that will allow you to endure and to keep pressing forward. It is that same internal presence that will build a hedge of protection around you and will defend you against your enemies. Trials are inevitable and some will even appear as insurmountable, which is why you have to possess an internal presence that is indestructible. Whenever you experience a personal storm in your life, God is your source of peace.

> "³³ 'These things I have spoken to you, that in Me you may have peace. In the world you will have tribulation; but be of good cheer, I have overcome the world.'" (John 16:33, NKJV)

You must worship God because of who He is, and not because of what He has done. When you worship God for who He is, then you recognize His power and sovereignty. The mere presence of God is enough reason for you to stand strong against any opposition in your life. The internal presence of God does not declare you as exempt from tribulation, but does declare you as equipped to handle tribulation. When your struggle seems too overwhelming, you may find yourself wanting to host a "pity party" and to offer a quick resignation. Instead of having a party to serve cups of despair and hors d'oeuvres of defeat, let the internal presence of God be your emcee and change the theme of your party.

Front-row Seat

When you hear that ticket sales are open for your favorite artist, how do you go about obtaining a ticket for the show? With the exception of a standing-room only ticket, the ticket will contain a section, row, and individual seat assignment. How many hours are you willing to spend camping outside, standing in line, or waiting on the phone to get a seat that is in the front row or as close as possible to the stage? Personally, I am quick to express my willingness to pay extra money for the front row.

Furthermore, I feel extra special whenever I obtain a front-row seat or a seat in the VIP section. Because of my determination to be as close as possible to the stage, I have camped outside overnight, stood in countless lines, and spent several hours on the phone for a variety of shows. I know that my enjoyment and level of participation are increased by the location of my seat. Along with that, a front-row seat enhances my experience because I feel like I can establish a personal connection with the performer.

I reference the entire row in this analogy because a row allows for multiple occupants. To further expound on my analogy, I want you to imagine that the performance stage represents your life, and that thousands of rows face the stage. I ask, "Where is your seat?" I believe that the location of your seat is directly correlated to the way that you love yourself. At first thought, you may respond that you are seated in the front row of the best section. With respect to the stage as your life, you should assess your view and level of connection. Perhaps, you will find that the location of your seat has an obstructed view or even has you sitting adjacent to the wrong person. The level of connection accounts for how well you know your purpose, and if you are working toward fulfilling your purpose.

Previously, I had heard my pastor make the comment that not every person in your circle was deserving of a seat in the front row of your life. I was in so much agreement with that comment that I began to scroll through the contact list in my phone. I considered the people that were in my life at that time and started to mark off the names of the people that I felt were in need of a seat reassignment. Audaciously, I decided which people were going to be relocated to the "nosebleed section" of my life. I also created a section near the exit door for those people that I had decided would need to be eradicated from my life.

I truly believed that I was seated in the front row of the VIP section, but I did not equate the performance stage to my life at that time. After I envisioned the performance stage as my life, I realized that I was actually sitting in the "nosebleed section" so I was not in a position to relocate anyone from my list. The truth was that I was so consumed with having a front-row seat at every other show that I needed high-definition binoculars to see what was really happening at my own show. In reality, I had spent more time trying to be number one in someone else's life that I did not notice the high altitude of the position that I occupied in my life.

My front-row seat analogy was a piercing wake-up call for me because I saw my life through a different lens. I discovered that what I had been calling clarity was really confusion, and what I had believed to be potential was really poisonous. I quickly realized that the distance between my seat and the stage had opened the door to greater obstructions. Consequently, the many obstructions caused a modification in the direction of my view. My focus was extremely congested, and my priorities were out of order.

The obvious disadvantage that accompanies the lack of having a front-row seat is that many other people are closer to the performance stage. When considering my front-row seat analogy, the enemy also had several options for a better seat, which enabled the enemy to cause more destruction in my life. I knew that I could not continue to allow the enemy to have a better seat than me in my own life. As a result, I decided to redefine myself, and the first step was the reassignment of my seat. Seeing the performance stage as my life, I kindly escorted myself down to the front row of the VIP section.

I was overcome with enthusiasm and anticipation as my outlook became clearer to me. I finally understood the reasons for my misinterpretation, misuse, and misplacement of love. For years, I had been looking for a man to protect me and to be my savior. I wanted a man to come to my defense and make me feel secure. I wanted a man to see beauty in me and love me unconditionally. With a better view of my life, I discovered that I had been trying to find a man that would replace the innocence that was stolen from me and heal my brokenness.

In other words, I realized that I had been expecting a man to do what only God could do for me. I finally allowed God to completely heal my emotional wounds instead of searching for another temporary bandage. I grew closer to God and had a new direction toward fulfilling my purpose. Moreover, I experienced the renewal of my soul and loved myself from the inside-out for the first time since I was a young girl. By occupying a front-row seat in my own life, I no longer felt the need to sketch my beauty so I stopped wearing my mask.

> "[2] The LORD is my rock and my fortress and my deliverer; My God, my strength, in whom I will trust; My shield and the horn of my salvation, my stronghold." (Psalm 18:2, NKJV)

God will always work on your behalf and will never ask you for time off. You have to trust God to seat the right people in the right seats. With God as an usher in your life, He will even seat an individual in the "nosebleed section" without you being aware. When you love yourself from the front row, only then can you begin the seat-relocation process for someone else in your life. The front-row seat is not a free pass for you to develop a superiority complex, but to allow you to have an unrestricted view of your life.

I summarize *LOVE* with the following scriptures:

> "¹⁴ I will praise You, for I am fearfully *and* wonderfully made; Marvelous are Your works, and *that* my soul knows very well." (Psalm 139:14, NKJV)

> "¹⁶ Therefore we do not lose heart. Even though our outward *man* is perishing, yet the inward man is being renewed day by day." (2 Corinthians 4:16, NKJV)

Chapter 2

INVEST

Investments are made to afford a multitude of things such as financial gain, security, wealth, education, equity, and ownership. For example, a 401k is a great way to save and prepare for retirement. As a means to establish ownership and build equity, the purchase of a home is commonly encouraged. The return on investment (ROI) is a popular measure and often used to evaluate the profitability of an investment. The cost and benefit are used to calculate the ROI. Regardless of the type of investment, a positive ROI is always a factor of motivation and influence.

The goal is to pursue an investment that will result in a profit, which includes monetary as well as non-monetary gain. As consumers, we acquire certain products based upon our individual standards and expected ROI. The ROI is not only important for tangible items, but the ROI is equally essential to your personal well-being and growth. When considering how people invest in themselves, I define the difference between the personal consumption of garbage and goals. I ask, "What are you feeding yourself?"

Garbage

By definition, garbage has no purpose, no significance, no substance, no use, and no value. Thus, the reasons why garbage is so easily discarded and not retained for a long period of time. Garbage is not sewn into soil and expected to reap a harvest. Garbage is not intended to be profitable and does not foster growth. To that point, garbage is not projected to have a positive ROI. Garbage can also cause an object to become deplorable as well as release a vile odor. Given the potential harm that garbage can impose on the body, garbage is considered unhealthy and should not be consumed by anyone.

Yet for over 20 years, I ingested garbage like the hatred toward my stepfather, the anger toward my father, the disrespect toward my mother, and the unforgiveness toward them all. I detested my stepfather for being an abusive tyrant and for destroying the self-worth of a young girl. I was enraged with my father for not saving me and for not being a source of protection. I disrespected my mother for bringing a tormentor into our home and for wearing what seemed to be a blindfold in the very volatile environment.

Unfortunately, the birth of my first brother did not relieve the abuse that my stepfather brought forth. I remember having to rescue my little brother from being punched, pushed, kicked, and thrown by my stepfather on so many occasions. At some point, I felt resentment toward my brother because I constantly had to protect him, but I did not have anyone to protect me. I learned to cope with the abuse by preparing myself to fight and by being determined to find a way out.

When my mother became pregnant with my second brother, I remember thinking that she was surely insane and not in her right mind. I saw the pregnancy as giving my stepfather another child to abuse, which was beyond what I could handle so my attitude toward my mother became worse. My level of disrespect toward her had become so egregious and unacceptable that my parents decided that I needed to live with my father instead of my mother. As a result of my relocation, I completely missed the birth of my second brother.

My gratitude and appreciation for being with family were diminished by the hatred that I had for my stepfather. I also know that my relationship with my brothers was severely hurt as a consequence. Because I began fueling my hatred at such a young age, I grew older without knowing how to love my brothers and detest their father at the same time so I chose to alienate myself from that side of my family. Unfortunately,

I did not take into account that my alienation would hinder the development of a bond between my brothers and me.

While growing up, my father had always allowed me to talk to him about anything, and no topic was off limits. At the same time, I never wanted to cause any hardship for my mother so I elected to remain silent about the abuse. Although I did not shy away from expressing my abhorrence of my stepfather, I kept the fact that I had been molested a secret from everyone until my early twenties. When I did share my experience, I provided the short version and avoided the intricate details. I was still very uncomfortable with talking about the abuse because of my disturbing memories and feeling of shame. My secret was uncovered, but I did not receive the closure from my parents that I had expected in return.

My mother made the choice to focus on raising my brothers and tried to provide a healthy home with my stepfather without tackling what he had done to me. My father chose not to confront my stepfather and moved forward as if the abuse had never taken place. Subsequently, I believed that my parents thought that I was lying because they both acted so disinterested about what I had suffered as a child. I also thought that the abuse was unaddressed by my parents because I was no longer a child and removed from the home with my stepfather. Physically, I was located in a much better place, but I was deep in emotional and psychological ruin. After I saw how my parents dealt with the disheartening discovery about me, I really questioned my personal worth and wondered if I would ever have anyone that cared enough to save me.

Years later, my father discovered that the daughter of his close friend had been molested and sexually assaulted by her stepfather. To my surprise, my father was the total opposite and spoke vehemently against that man. My father was extremely disgusted by the situation, and I wholeheartedly shared his sentiments. I was excited to know that my father was so supportive, but I was also hurt by the dichotomy of his reaction toward me. I had been molested before the other young lady, but it seemed as if my repulsive experience with my stepfather was only a problem for me.

I also remembered when my health had required me to have surgery, and my father was not present because he refused to take time off from work. My understanding was that my father would not use his personal time for anyone other than himself. On the contrary, my father was eager to take time off from work to attend the hearings that were related to the criminal case against that young lady's stepfather. While I empathized with that young lady, I could not help but to wonder about my father. I wondered what would make my father care so much about the molestation of another person's daughter, but ignore the molestation of his own daughter.

Subsequently, I wrote my thoughts and feelings in a letter to my father because I was not able to talk about the situation. Sadly, that letter resulted in more discouragement for me because my father was offended by the content of my letter. He never tried to understand the dispirited, but honest, place that my words had resonated from. Despite the abrasive words that my father said to me, he finally spoke to my stepfather about the abuse. I knew that the conversation between them was motivated by what I had said in the letter and not motivated by a father who was sincerely outraged by what had happened to his daughter. At that time, I was almost 30 years old and filled with enormous shame so I hardened myself even more to cope with the loss that continued to haunt me.

Depending on the circumstances, a person may be able to recover an item that was previously stolen. Unfortunately, I was robbed of my innocence as a child, which was something that I could never reclaim and never replace. The questions of why no one ever cared or did anything about the abuse that happened to me had caused me to become an untrusting and unforgiving woman. I literally refused to forgive my stepfather, father, and mother because I had defined forgiveness as permission to be violated. I had convinced myself that I needed to see them suffer miserably before I would even consider the topic of forgiveness for discussion. In retrospect, I am certain that no amount of suffering would have ever been acceptable in my sight. Thus, instead of undergoing a much-needed purge, my consumption of garbage continued to increase day after day.

Plastic Bag

I refer to the small plastic bags that are used to carry the items that are purchased in a store. Typically, the plastic bags are packed at the store, and then unpacked at home. Often times, an unpacked bag is assessed to determine its condition and its potential to be reused in the future. If the bag meets the standard, then the bag is commonly stored with other bags for the purpose of reuse. The plastic bag tends to offer a good amount of durability and affords a convenience for carrying a variety of items. The plastic bag is also made to be pliable, which enables the bag's ability to stretch.

As a caveat, the size of an item may possibly cause deformation to the shape of the plastic bag. Beyond that, the plastic bag may completely lose its structure and explode because of the weight of the load. Many people often reuse those plastic bags to serve as garbage bags. Nonetheless, the garbage will still be garbage regardless of its container. Once the garbage begins to corrode, the corroded material may cause the container to leak or develop a stench. When was the last time that you walked past a dumpster that had a refreshing scent? Overall, garbage represents any unwanted item that has been determined to be worthless.

As children of God, we were born with high value. Yet, many of God's children allow themselves to be altered in such a way that depreciates their personal value. In the past, I depreciated so much that I unintentionally imitated a plastic bag that was carrying garbage. I thought that my ability to carry a heavy burden was indicative of my elasticity and fortitude at work. In retrospect, I believe that I became more like a plastic bag as an attempt to protect myself.

For more than 20 years, I felt like I was in a war, but never had more than one person in my army. The garbage that I carried was like my ammunition that became a requirement for my survival. I say ammunition because I used my demoralizing memories and unforgiveness to attack others. I developed a calloused heart to limit my emotions, which also enabled me to be very guarded. Occasionally, I would try to lower my guard for the sake of having a healthier relationship with someone. With each failed relationship, I would consume more garbage like unforgiveness and bitterness to avoid getting too close to vulnerability. I truly wanted to have love in my life, but I did not want to have to be vulnerable to get it.

Furthermore, my state of being a plastic bag that was carrying garbage also caused me to have horrible nightmares for almost two decades. I still remember how my screaming and crying would wake me up from my sleep. My nightmares were always quite vivid and graphic depictions. The scenes were replays of what I had experienced at home with my stepfather and extreme portrayals of how I was really feeling about everyone. I would shout for help in my nightmares, but would always be ignored. In my nightmares, my mother would appear, but she was always detached and would remain at a distance. As for my stepfather, he would embody a raging giant with power over me.

My father was never present in any of my nightmares, which represented his physical and emotional distance from me. For me, my nightmares simply reproduced the abuse by my stepfather, and the feeling of abandonment by both of my parents. My nightmares continued long after I had left the home with my stepfather, which forced me to keep reliving those miserable moments over and over. Unfortunately, with such visual nightmares, the weight of the garbage that I carried just kept getting heavier over the years.

I present my analogy of a plastic bag to demonstrate how a valuable item could be modified to contain things that are of no value so much that the item becomes valueless itself. What was just a simple plastic bag had become a real-life comparison for me. When I examined my past, I saw how I had allowed myself to be stretched, torn, distorted, and busted wide open. I became comfortable with harboring such an unhealthy load because I wore it like armor for numerous years. I had even managed to convince myself that I was a stronger woman because I had carried so much weight. Eventually, I was harboring an excessive amount of garbage and did not fully recognize the implications of its weight until I had an emotional explosion.

No Progress

Garbage is susceptible to decomposition, which prevents any form of further growth. When you hold on to garbage like anger, unforgiveness, hurt, shame, or hatred, you are allowing your previous experience to keep you in a state of imprisonment. You may be a hoarder of this type of garbage because you are waiting for that person to pay the price for their wrongdoing against you. While you are waiting to see the suffering of another person, the truth is that you are stunting your own progress. The wheels of your life are spinning, but you will remain stationary. The seeds of your life are planted, but you will not blossom. The clock of your life is ticking, but your season will not change.

I remember when I obtained my own apartment at age 19 and started my independent voyage. At 19, I did believe that I was in control of my life and headed toward fulfilling my destiny. Years later, I realized that I had spent a lot of time being lost and lacked a consistent connection to God. I recognized that I could not receive any guidance from God as long as I continued to interfere by carrying so much hatred and unforgiveness. Basically, the "plastic bag" that I became to defend myself against other people had eventually become the same barricade that also hindered my relationship with God. It was as if I only knew of Him by way of the stories that I had heard, but I really did not know Him for myself. I would say, "God is good!" but I was just repeating the words of my grandmother. To my surprise, I had been totally independent and living on my own, but I was also in a place of stagnation.

Many people make the mistake of trying to share the responsibility of their problems with God. How many times have you decided to put your problem in God's hands, but then continued to try to resolve the problem on your own? I consider that as a case of casting the problem while remaining connected to the problem. For example, a fisherman uses the reel that is mounted on a fishing rod to retain, release, or retract the fishing line. The bait is attached to the hook at the end of the fishing line. In the sport of fishing, the bait is used to lure and to catch fish. When you treat your problems like bait, then your catch will only consist of more problems. To cast while remaining connected is what I define as going to God with a clenched fist instead of an open hand. Thus, a person with a clenched fist is holding on to garbage and will have limited progress.

When you allow your body to be a resting place for your garbage, you are subjecting your health to decay and will hinder your ability to move forward. The problems from your past experiences are not meant to be stored and carried as luggage. The garbage that you carry is a hindrance to you and to God as well. God wants to work through you, but He cannot use you as a vessel while you are in a state of no progression. You have to recognize that you cannot carry the loads of your past and consider yourself to be full steam ahead at the same time. When you go to God, you must release your problem to Him by casting without remaining connected to your problem. Ultimately, you will eliminate what is working against you and make room for what is working for you.

Goals

A goal represents the desired outcome that you are working to achieve and should be specific, realistic, and time-sensitive. A well-defined goal helps to prevent ambiguity and ensures focus on exactly what needs to be done. Also, a goal has to be realistic as well as challenging to help support motivation and maintain momentum. The assignment of a target date for completion imposes necessary constraints and enforces greater accountability in regard to a goal. In a workplace, the performance of an employee is often measured against the goals that were set forth in the beginning. The establishment of a goal is very beneficial and useful in every aspect of a person's life.

Planned Purpose

Many people are confident about their purpose, while others admit to not having a clue about their purpose. I equate the goal to the "what" you are striving to achieve and equate the purpose to the "why" you are striving to achieve. Commonly, goals are categorized as short-term and long-term and help a person to stay on course with an associated plan. I believe that your goals should be linked to your God-given purpose. When you connect your goals to the purpose that God has given you, you place yourself in alignment with God's plan for your life.

As described by my analogy of a plastic bag, you can reuse an item to serve another purpose, but think about the original purpose that the item was created to fulfill. When a quick solution is needed, I think we are all guilty of reusing an item that will work for a different purpose other than what that item was originally built to serve. The opportunity to reuse something is much easier when that item lends itself to being repurposed. If an item is determined to be workable for a different use, then that item will most likely be repurposed. Personally, I find myself storing things because of my confidence to make that item work for another purpose in the future.

With that being said, do not fall into the trap of being a "this will work" classification and allow yourself to be depreciated by being used for the wrong purpose. I believe that you can serve more than one purpose, but your work should be based on a firm foundation and not a sinkhole. A firm foundation will help ensure that you are following the plan that God has destined for you. Furthermore, you must never allow yourself to mimic a plastic bag that is holding garbage. Even though you may think that you can just "double bag" yourself to become more resilient, you will eventually break because you are carrying too much weight. God has the ultimate plan for you so you must surrender yourself to the purpose that He has for your life.

> "[21] There are many plans in a man's heart, Nevertheless the LORD's counsel – that will stand." (Proverbs 19:21, NKJV)

> "[28] And we know that all things work together for good to those who love God, to those who are the called according to *His* purpose." (Romans 8:28, NKJV)

In my early thirties, I finally decided to let go of the garbage that I had been carrying for so many years and put it in its proper place. I was tired of trying to declare my own purpose and trying to convince God that my plan was best. While I had been successful in wearing my mask, I still had an emotional void that kept me in a state of exhaustion. I knew that I needed to be healed before I could really connect with God and have a better relationship with Him. I had to release the distrust, hatred, disrespect, and unforgiveness so that God's purpose could reign in my life.

After my introspection, I accepted that forgiveness was my only answer. The same forgiveness that I had ostracized and cursed was what opened the door to my healing. I finally stretched my open hand to God and felt immediate liberation from the garbage that had kept me bound for so many years. Without having a conversation with any of them, I forgave my stepfather, mother, and father for the role that they each played in regard to the abuse that I had gone through. By way of forgiveness, my awful nightmares instantly disappeared, and my dreams became experiences of tranquility.

> "[22] Cast your burden on the LORD, And He shall sustain you; He shall never permit the righteous to be moved." (Psalm 55:22, NKJV)

Later, when I found myself besieged with depression again, I questioned whether or not I had been healed from my abuse. I remember looking in the mirror and arguing with myself because I thought that I had a lucid understanding of God's purpose for my life. While I had felt a renewed spirit before, I realized that I was still shackled to shame. I had frequently heard God tell me to testify about how He had delivered me, but I wanted that part of me to remain hidden. As a result, I had coined myself as a "closet praiser" because I would only praise God about being delivered from molestation behind closed doors.

The resurfacing of my struggle with shame and guilt enabled me to realize that I still had one more person to forgive, which was myself. Finally, I forgave myself and said goodbye to the shame that had kept me silent in the dark for more than two decades. On that day, glory to God, I began to openly praise God and never wore the face of shame again. The darkness was behind me, and I definitively knew the purpose that God had for my life. Subsequently, my mask became nothing more than a figure of my past, and I moved forward with the *L.I.V.E. Commitment.*

God's Blueprint

When considering a blueprint, it is always a tailored and traceable guide for a particular design. A blueprint outlines the details of a plan from start to finish and supports the final product. In the past, I tried using my own blueprint because I was confident in the skills that I had developed. I thought that my personal experiences were sufficient evidence to support that I knew how to handle and overcome adversity. Also, I was certain that my way of resolving a problem was the best in many instances.

For example, I had confirmation that God had not chosen Raider as the man for me within six months of dating him. Despite Raider's blatant lies, I still thought that I could save him and cure him of his dishonesty. He had lied about everything from his children to where he lived to what he owned, but I believed that I could help free him from being immersed in deception. I thought that I had enough influence and power to make Raider become a better man so I kept his lies a secret. Truthfully, I thought that I could prove God wrong when considering that case.

I knew that Raider's struggles were not just because of his financial deficiencies, but I discovered that many of his struggles were consequences of how he loved himself. He was insecure and preferred to surround himself with people that made him feel superior like the outside-in type of person. Sadly, I felt like a total failure when I witnessed the extreme measures that Raider had taken to perpetuate his duplicity. I was both astounded and disheartened to be a witness to one of his many domestic battles. Later, I realized that Raider's need to feel superior meant more to him than the lacerations to his face.

While I was so focused on changing Raider for the better, I was in fact losing myself and trying to operate on an empty tank. I tried to make sense of my blueprint that had been figuratively shredded to pieces. After several futile attempts, I felt like I had been slapped in the face with a 747 airplane, and I completely blamed God for it all. My conversation with God went like this: I screamed, "Really? God, how could you just let this foolishness happen to me? You are omniscient so you knew that this was coming! What in the world are You doing up there?"

God replied to me with a calm and formal tone, "Well Dr. Williams, I beeped the horn, flashed hazard lights, increased the stop signs, added road blocks, cancelled the trip, threw a flag, called time out, put you on the bench, rang the alarm, sent a storm, and shook your foundation, but you chose to ignore every single warning that I presented to you. Girl, get somewhere and sit down because this conversation is over!" I could not believe that I heard God use a phrase that I had often used so I sat down and did it quickly.

The fact that God had spoken to me with such a tone of composure made me reconsider my placement of anger and blame. Thus, I found myself in a position where I had to admit my own participation in the events that resulted in my emotional explosion. I realized how easy it had been to point the finger at someone else and declare that other person as having fault. Sure, you can point your finger at someone else, but are you able to point your finger at yourself? The nature of having to accept responsibility for the role that you played in hurting someone else is often a challenge, but it is even more difficult to accept responsibility for the role that you played in bringing hurt upon yourself. After acknowledging the significant number of warning signs that I had ignored, I was compelled to accept the consequences that resulted from using my own self-made blueprint. To that point, I had to recognize how I was responsible for opening the door to some of my heartache.

Unfortunately, I spent years in various unhealthy relationships because I chose not to follow God. I asked God for guidance and He gave me the correct instructions on countless occasions, but I was not a consistent team player. I wanted God to be "on call" for me and to play according to my rules. Along with my rules, I also wanted God to cater to my emotions. As humans, our personal attributes like our decisions, thoughts, and actions can be easily clouded by our emotions. God is not predicated upon human emotions and is not constrained by human boundaries. At times, many of us are guilty of trying to force God into a role that He has already declined because we are so determined to obey our own script. Even when our personal agenda appears to be impeccable, God's blueprint is the only blueprint that meets perfection. God will know before you know and will see before you see so He will always own the master blueprint.

> "⁸ I will instruct you and teach you in the way you should go; I will guide you with My eye." (Psalm 32:8, NKJV)

> "⁸ 'For My thoughts *are* not your thoughts, Nor *are* your ways My ways,' says the LORD. ⁹ 'For *as* the heavens are higher than the earth, So are My ways higher than your ways, And My thoughts than your thoughts.'" (Isaiah 55:8-9, NKJV)

When God gives you a purpose, He also provides you with a custom-made blueprint to help you fulfill that purpose. You are not expected to traverse aimlessly, which is why you have direct access to the best pilot in the world. God's blueprint is always personalized for each individual and cannot be found in a repository online. If designed by God, one person's blueprint cannot be duplicated to become applicable for another person. Whatever God has for you, is for you, which includes your unique blueprint to connect to your purpose. You should never rely on your self-made or another person's blueprint, but you should only depend on God's blueprint to help guide you through the process.

I summarize *INVEST* with the following scriptures:

> "⁷ Do not be not deceived, God is not mocked; for whatever a man sows, that he will also reap." (Galatians 6:7, NKJV)

> "⁵ 'I am the vine, you *are* the branches. He who abides in Me, and I in him, bears much fruit; for without Me you can do nothing.'" (John 15:5, NKJV)

Chapter 3

VICTORY

The Global Positioning System (GPS) is known as a satellite-based navigation system that provides users with positioning, navigation, and timing services. Undoubtedly, GPS is a great solution when you need directions in advance to a particular address, you are lost in a strange place, or you want to know an alternate route. Today, GPS technology is conveniently available on a plethora of devices and accessible at a person's fingertips. Given the convenience of GPS, many people use it as their primary source for directions to ensure successful arrival to a location. A number of people have become rather dependent on their GPS and dare to leave home without it. Despite the fact that GPS is not 100% accurate, many of us still trust and seek our GPS system for assistance. I ask, "How do you use GPS?"

Divine GPS

From an early age, I was taught to take responsibility for my problems by resolving them on my own. As I grew into adulthood, I believed that asking for help was a sign of weakness because my father had imbued me with independence and more independence. He insisted that I learned how to survive on my own, as preparation in the case that I remained single. I recall the times when my father saw me walking on the highway headed home, but he did not feel like switching lanes so he drove past me. He taught me to only rely on myself in order to ensure success. Also, my father was adamant about me having a detailed plan for everything and did not ever allow a lackadaisical attitude.

In addition to what I was taught while growing up, I also trained myself to operate as a solo act because I did not have the support that I needed during the most hurtful times in my life. I convinced myself that dependence on another person meant sadness and disappointment so I refused to be in a position to ever need anyone. As a result, I decided that I would only allow myself to want a person in my life and not actually need a person in my life. I had believed that my philosophy would help to minimize my emotional attachment to others. My idea of "want vs. need" became a driving force that I used to help navigate through the paths in my life, and the people along the way.

I despised being lost and unable to find my own way even though I had a tendency to step outside of my comfort zone. As a result, I would frequently spend a significant amount of time trying to figure out a problem on my own because I chose not to seek guidance. I would often stretch my personal limits because I had a solid plan for success; at least that was what I consistently thought. My father had applauded me so much for being completely self-sufficient that being anything less was a challenge for me.

Furthermore, I had also learned to accept my father's position on certain topics. If I discussed a financial problem with my father, he would tell me to figure it out. If I discussed an emotional problem with my father, he would tell me to toughen up. Eventually, I began to chastise myself for being "too soft" or for allowing any type of problem to test my nerves. With my ambition to be a superwoman, I had reached a point where the idea of needing to enlist someone's assistance for a problem was more disturbing to me than the problem itself. While I truly appreciated the many survival skills that my father had inspired me to develop, I also knew that I had formed a strong opposing attitude toward any form of dependency on another person.

At one time, I was dealing with several struggles that covered my finances, emotions, and health. I had so many issues attacking me at the same time that I was losing my mind trying to resolve each one on my own. I was faced with so much uncertainty that I felt like all of my advance preparation had become futile. Finally, I accepted that my crusade to be a superwoman was a perilous mission, and that I needed help in order to move forward on the correct path. I realized that God had been with me since the beginning, and that every delay was not His denial. I made several deviations that had taken me away from the correct path, but God stepped in and saved me from myself every time. While having God as my guide, I was headed in the direction of victory because I had discovered an even greater GPS.

As an alternative to technology, I propose what I call *divine GPS* for guidance, which I define as "God's Provision for Success." While the technical GPS is definitely a valuable asset, I believe that everyone should also keep an active account of *divine GPS* at all times. This unique kind of GPS will provide you with the strength and insight that you cannot acquire on your own or from technology. Also, God is not device-dependent because He never needs to be downloaded or upgraded. You have to trust God to be your pilot without trying to be His co-pilot. There is no better source to use for direction than God, and there is no better path to success than the path that is laid by Him. Remember, you have to trust God and try God; try God and trust God!

> "⁵ Trust in the LORD with all your heart, And lean not on your own understanding; ⁶ In all your ways acknowledge Him, And He shall direct your paths." (Proverbs 3:5-6, NKJV)

Given my new approach to victory, I recognized that a person's testimony does not come by being a hoarder of conflict, but by releasing the conflict and letting God be God. Although you may feel like you reside in distress, do not give your trouble a permanent address in your life. You may experience a detour along your journey, which is why you must allow God to combine His super with your natural to ensure that you are directed by the best source. With your *divine GPS* in control, you will always arrive at the right location, and at the right time. The use of technology will never outsmart God because He is the only perfect source. The awesome news about God is that He is never restricted by bandwidth, never affected by construction, never hindered by inclement weather, never dropped by the loss of a signal, never going to say "Can you hear me now?" and never going to lose power.

Victim to Victor

On many occasions, I would sit in the sanctuary of my church and belt out a scream so loud that I believe that the people in the next city could have heard me. I would feel the Holy Spirit, but would sit motionless like I was strapped to my seat. I would not talk about what had me bound, but I would just scream and scream and scream some more. The reality is that when you inhale garbage, you will exhale unproductive things like anger, depression, unforgiveness, and defeat.

For some people, the place of being a victim can become a place of complacency. You may feel like your struggle is not going to change so you accept your struggle as being normal. For many years, I used my abuse as a crutch to justify my unkind behavior and harsh tongue toward others. The thought of forgiveness was like opening the door to destruction so I vowed to keep a hardened heart. Furthermore, I allowed my shame and guilt to make me feel that I would never be more than just a victim, as if it were stamped on my forehead. My desires, emotions, and actions were constantly affected by the fact that I had believed that I would never overcome the state of being a victim.

During my self-evaluation, I recognized that I had also been guilty of misinterpreting, misusing, and misplacing love. I realized that my understanding of love was extremely warped and included many misrepresentations. Unfortunately, I had perplexed feelings about how to love my parents because their love for me seemed to be inhibited. Although my mother's love for me was unconditional for the most part, the "elephant in the room" regarding my stepfather posed an enormous strain on my relationship with her. My father's love was conditional and dependent on my successes so I often felt like I was living just to obtain his approval. Also, I was unclear about the image of what love looked like between a man and a woman.

For several years, my desire to date a man was subject to my simple rule of the thumb. I would figuratively divide the new man by the previous man to obtain a "thumbs up" or "thumbs down" indication. Based upon my thumb rule, I would date a man because I thought that he was better than the previous man was for me, but not because I thought that he was the best man for me. My principles for dating were merely based on trial and error without having any substance. By having such inferior principles, I believe that I misconstrued the quality of my relationships. I also noticed that the same problems kept appearing in every relationship, and I would always look at the man as the one at fault.

Have you ever felt like you were dealing with an everlasting problem? At times, a person may wonder about the status of their problem and cannot comprehend why their problem is still lingering around. Too often, many of us are guilty of giving permanent status to something or someone that was intended to only be temporary. Worry is a way to give long-lasting residency to a problem that should have been vacated or to give life to a problem that has yet to present itself. Beyond that, I had to understand that not every problem in my life was a matter of God's way, but some of my problems were a result of my own permission. For example, the times when God closed the door to my problem, but I opened a window and let the problem back in. I adopted a "fixer" mentality because I had believed in that being the mindset to give me more control in my life. I always thought that if I could just fix the problem according to my own plan, then I would have the success that was meant for me.

After many years of trial and error in multiple facets of my life, I became more obedient to God's guidance and adhered to His instructions to find victory. I trusted God to be the ultimate "fixer" and stopped trying to solve all of my problems on my own. I stopped bombarding my mind with worry about the tribulations that I had encountered because I knew that God's resolution would not fail. In addition, I accepted that it was not possible for every man that I dated to have the exact same problem. I finally stopped blaming men for every unsuccessful relationship and took ownership of my responsibility so that I could address my genuine struggles.

The idea of facing my personal struggles was daunting at first, but an assignment that I knew had to be done. I made the decision to forgive, and I let go of my grasp to the past. When I forgave the person that abused me, I did not forget about the abuse that was done to me, but I freed myself from decades of shame. The power of forgiveness allowed me to live victoriously. I realized that forgiveness does not equal emotional failure, but forgiveness does equal emotional freedom. The day that I fired the victim in me and hired the victor in me was the day that I embraced my authenticity. I no longer desired to have what was just better for me, but I desired to only have what was best for me.

> "⁵⁷ But thanks *be* to God, who gives us the victory through our Lord Jesus Christ." (1 Corinthians 15:57, NKJV)

> "⁸ Oh, taste and see that the LORD *is* good; Blessed *is* the man *who* trusts in Him!" (Psalm 34:8, NKJV)

When you change your position from victim to victor, you transition away from being consumed by defeat. A defeatist mindset is the work of the enemy to pin you against yourself. The enemy wants you to remain in a victimized state so you have to strengthen your mind and employ yourself with the role of a victor. With God, you are more than a conqueror and victory abides within you. You must remember that God already has the solution before you ever have the problem, which is why the *L.I.V.E. Commitment* requires you to find victory in yourself and not by yourself.

I summarize *VICTORY* with the following scriptures:

> "⁴ You are of God, little children, and have overcome them, because He who is in you is greater than he who is in the world." (1 John 4:4, NKJV)

> "⁹ And He said to me, 'My grace is sufficient for you, for My strength is made perfect in weakness.' Therefore most gladly I will rather boast in my infirmities, that the power of Christ may rest upon me. ¹⁰ Therefore I take pleasure in infirmities, in reproaches, in needs,

in persecutions, in distresses, for Christ's sake. For when I am weak, then I am strong." (2 Corinthians 12:9-10, NKJV)

Chapter 4

ENCOURAGE

Mirror Reflection

A mirror is commonly used to show a reflection of something or someone. Also, mirrors can be found in a multitude of shapes and sizes. When shopping for clothes, a mirror allows the consumer to get a real-time view of how the clothing will look on the consumer. The majority of bathrooms, private and public, contain some type of mirror. Automobiles are equipped with mirrors to aid the driver with seeing what is located behind or alongside of the driver's automobile. The use of a mirror may change based upon the particular needs of an individual. Personally, I learned to use my mirror to see more than just my current appearance. In fact, I discovered that a mirror can provide a reflection of both my present and past. I ask, "What does your reflection mean to you?"

Duplicate Your Present

More often than not, people use a mirror to help with personal aesthetics. When you look into a mirror, you immediately see the duplication of your physical appearance. A mirror is the best way to know exactly what you are presenting to the public. A mirror will confirm when you are looking like what I call a 300-degree mess and will give you a clear view of what needs to be corrected. Ultimately, a mirror helps to ensure that you look the way that you want to look. In addition to providing you with a duplication of yourself, I believe that a mirror can also help to tell your story.

A mirror can be used to reflect upon your "now" and allow you to think about what is currently going on in your life. The reflection should be inclusive of both the positive and negative circumstances that are current in your life. With this in mind, I am not suggesting that you should actually look like your current situation. For example, if you are financially wealthy, that does not mean that your forehead should be painted with diamonds. Conversely, if you are unemployed, that does not mean that you should look busted and disgusted. Of course, a praise party is so much easier when everything is going well for you. The more difficult task is to praise God even when the road is pitch black and misfortune seems to ride upon your heels.

Until my late thirties, I would look into the mirror and only see a broken woman that was inundated with guilt and shame. Even though I thought that my healing had to come from a man, I dealt with my emotions by hardening myself like a concrete wall. My puzzling solution to healing was to be a callus and limit the permeation of additional heartache. I became an adult who was shaped by the shame that I carried because I had been molested as a child. I did not know how to encourage myself because I could not see beyond the darkness that had surrounded me for what had seemed like forever. I was so focused on what was negative that I lost sight of what was positive.

I failed to praise God for the simple things like the breath in my lungs, and the dawning of a new day. Basically, it was if I walked around with the enemy sitting right on my shoulder and speaking directly into my ear. For many years, I allowed the enemy to convince me that my troubles outweighed my triumphs so my "now" consisted of a constant spiritual battle within me. I had to recognize that my current situation could be changed as long as God was in control. Once I acknowledged God as my complete sustainer, I saw the reflection of a woman who had been restored instead of the fragmented soul of a little girl.

Despite the perpetuating hurdles that may exist, you need to trust that God has the power to renovate your circumstances so encourage yourself to keep pressing forward. The enemy is in the recruiting business and seeks to maintain a full roster. Thus, the enemy is always nearby and trying to distract you from reaching your destiny. You have to brush the enemy off of your shoulder in such a way that the enemy is crushed underneath your feet. Even if you see the clouds begin to thicken and hear the thunder begin to rumble, do not forfeit or be dismayed by what may be ahead of you. Instead, you must encourage yourself through the storm and make the enemy distraught. You should praise God so loud that the enemy says, "WTH!" Regardless of the state of your "now" situation, you must stand firm on the Word of God and always be encouraged.

> "⁸ *We are* hard-pressed on every side, yet not crushed; *we are* perplexed, but not in despair; ⁹ persecuted, but not forsaken; struck down, but not destroyed--" (2 Corinthians 4:8-9, NKJV)

Recall Your Past

In addition to your present state, I believe that a mirror can also provide you with the opportunity to recall your "before" and reflect upon your past experiences. You are the only person that knows all of the details about your transformation, and all of what God has done for you. You may have family or friends that know you well, but they do not know every minor and major detail of your life. At some point, we have all had thoughts or committed actions that we have elected not to share with anyone. You may even experience that some people just want to remind you of your past in an attempt to keep you stagnant and block your progress. I am not suggesting that you should seek to relive your past, but I believe that you can use your past to acknowledge and to appreciate your own growth.

Since I had been molested as a child, I used to believe that I should have been automatically exempt from any further tests. I repeatedly said to God, "Why must I continue to be tested? My testimony does not need any additional building because it is good as it is!" Even when I had already experienced victory in so many ways, I would continue to doubt my ability to be a conqueror again. I was so afraid that one day I would encounter an obstacle that I could not overcome that I would allow my fear to affect my faith.

No matter how much I had achieved, I kept feeling like I could not get away from distress and discomfort. I would get discouraged and be reminded of the popular adage that says, "If God did it before, then He will do it again!" I had to learn to use my "before" to reinforce my "now" because I found myself treating repeat obstacles like they were "first-timers" in my life. I realized that walking with God was not an indication that my life would be without any obstacles, but walking with God was an indication that I possessed the means to overcome such obstacles.

The enemy is always eavesdropping and tries to stay one step ahead of you. Furthermore, the enemy is tenacious and will create distractions that are tailored just for you. Because the enemy does know your taste, you may observe similarity between some of your problems. You may feel like you are facing the same problem over and over again. Whenever you experience a "repeat-offender" type of problem, you have to pat yourself on the back and tell the enemy, "been there, done that!"

In addition, you have to learn from your past and look for the blessing in every situation. For example, the blessing may be that you received a severance package even though you lost your job. The blessing may be that your relationship terminated before you ended up in an unhealthy marriage. Often times, the thought of seeing the positive in a very negative situation seems like an impossible task. You can easily miss a blessing because you expect your blessing to be adorned according to your personal standards. In the past, I thought that I knew exactly what my blessings would look like so I struggled with yielding to God when His plan did not match mine. After I realigned myself with God, I began to operate according to His plan and stopped trying to dictate how my blessings would be bestowed upon me.

Of course, we have all experienced things like disappointments, setbacks, obstacles, heartaches, but we do not have to wear the issues of our past. You have to leave your past behind you and not carry your past forward so that you can experience growth in your life. In other words, do not allow your past to become your present because you refuse to let go. I am not advocating you to develop a sense of arrogance, but you are more than a conqueror with God fighting your battles.

God has never failed you so let the reflection of your "before" be a source of reassurance. God was God yesterday, God is God today, and God will be God tomorrow. When you look back over your life, you see that none of your past problems were able to defeat God so you have to remember that the same holds true for your future.

> "² My brethren, count it all joy when you fall into various trials, ³ knowing that the testing of your faith produces patience." (James 1:2-3, NKJV)

Two-Dimensional Network

I believe that an individual's personal network is two-dimensional and should consist of both horizontal and vertical planes in order to be complete. A network is a group of at least two items, and an interconnection must exist between those items. In this case, I am talking about people that have an interconnection in order to establish a network. The degree of interconnection between the people may vary across a network.

Regarding your own personal network, you should always assess your horizontal and vertical planes. I have heard some people brag about who is in their network. Furthermore, I have also heard some people boast about the coverage area of their network. The circumference or number of interconnected people within your personal network is not a direct measure of your network's strength. More importantly, your network is not worth boasting about if it lacks reliability. I ask, "How reliable is your network?"

At an early age, I was very determined to do everything on my own and developed an analytical approach. Eventually, I became a first-generation college student, and my mother was the primary person that encouraged me to pursue my bachelor's degree. My freshman year was quite difficult for me, which placed a lot of doubt in the mind of my father. I dropped out of college and worked multiple jobs to support myself over the next three years in Pennsylvania. When I decided to transfer to college in North Carolina, my mother believed that I would graduate, but my father believed that I would fail. I moved into the dorm and did not have enough money to return home to Pennsylvania. I was alone in North Carolina and wondered if I had taken my "do it on my own" campaign too far. I soon became best friends with my roommate and added to the horizontal plane of my network.

Surprisingly, when I needed money in North Carolina, my stepfather was very helpful even though he and I did not have any type of a relationship. Unfortunately, my father barely talked to me and refused to give me financial support during my matriculation in North Carolina. I never understood how my stepfather and father had seemingly switched roles about encouraging me. My stepfather, who used to tell me that I would never be more than a "spoiled bitch," said that he was proud of me for being an amazing and intelligent woman. My father, who used to push me to dream big and excel, told me that college was not for me and that I was not suited to be an engineer. Yet again, I felt like my father had deserted me in a foreign place, but this time I was more prepared to take the journey by myself.

Although I was extremely disappointed that I did not have unconditional support from my father, I used my emotions as fuel to propel me forward. I was determined to succeed and to improve the outlook of my future. I funded my undergraduate education with student loans, a host of fellowships, and summer internships. I enrolled in a full load of classes each semester and maintained a great amount of discipline to ensure my success. One of my professors, who became like a father to me, was a positive reinforcement that helped me to focus on advancing my education. I truly wanted to be an inspiration to others, and I wanted to prove that I could overcome the "naysayers" in my life.

While pursuing my bachelor's degree, I had established a network that consisted of family, friends, professors, colleagues, and mentors. I was confident that my horizontal plane was solid and represented a stable building block. But, unfortunately, my horizontal plane also experienced a significant amount of fluctuation as well. I struggled with the fact that my horizontal plane did not afford a high level of consistency and reciprocation from others. Since I had handpicked the people in my horizontal plane, I actually thought that I would have greater victories. Retrospectively, I believe that my overall expectation of my horizontal plane led to many of the problems that I continued to face. I wanted my horizontal plane to heal all of my emotional wounds and to fill the void in my life. In essence, I felt damaged so I expected my network to be a source of restoration, but I was relying on the wrong plane to do all of the work.

When we are faced with a problem, many of us tend to look out to our horizontal plane for help. Often times, we want to call on someone who is tangible and physically available to be in our presence. As the horizontal plane of a network is a great resource that the majority of people proudly use, the interconnections are not guaranteed to offer a lifetime of reliability. The challenge is that the horizontal plane of your network is subject to closures, potholes, expenses, and breakdowns. The fact that some of your most appreciated interconnections may become fickle or even non-existent is a tough reality. Furthermore, your horizontal plane is also susceptible to the "bandwagoners" who will want your testimony, but not your test. Simply stated, your horizontal plane will always contain flaws because it is a human interconnection.

On the contrary, the vertical plane of your network is inherently perfect and without fault. When you think about your vertical plane, it is God and God alone. God is omniscient so He does not need to ask you for your opinion. God is omnipotent so He does not need to ask you for your help. God is omnipresent so He does not need to ask you for a ride. God does not possess characteristics like mood swings, convenient amnesia, or pretenses. Another benefit is the fact that the vertical plane does not have an interconnection fee. Beyond that, God offers the only interconnection that you will ever have that will remain unchanged. Unlike the horizontal plane, the vertical plane has a guaranteed solution to every one of your problems because God cannot be defeated.

> "[1] God *is* our refuge and strength, A very present help in trouble." (Psalm 46:1, NKJV)

We should all have a personal network that is comprised of both a horizontal plane and a vertical plane because each plane serves its own purpose. As you operate in both planes, you have to nurture all of your interconnections and maintain your own level of accountability across your entire network. When you prioritize your vertical or virtuous plane to be first, then God will help you to establish your horizontal or human plane.

In support of encouragement, you have to foster interconnections that are productive and not destructive. Despite the people that may exist in your horizontal plane, the strength and power of your vertical plane is unparalleled. The difference is that only your vertical plane can stand on its own and offer you the gift of eternal life. With God in your network, you will always be connected to mercy and grace so you always have a reason to praise and to be encouraged.

I summarize *ENCOURAGE* with the following scriptures:

> "[28] 'Come to Me, all *you* who labor and are heavy laden, and I will give you rest.'" (Matthew 11:28, NKJV)

> "[31] But those who wait on the Lord Shall renew *their* strength; They shall mount up with wings like eagles, They shall run and not be weary, They shall walk and not faint." (Isaiah 40:31, NKJV)

CONCLUSION

After years of being like a garbage bag, I forgave everyone, including myself, and claimed the victory that God had for me. My past of being molested did not haunt me anymore so I dropped my mask and did not turn back. I was freed from my bondage so I had no reason to bow to shame ever again. I learned to praise and to thank God for my testimony because it confirms His magnificent role in my life.

With boundless joy, I can say that I no longer engage in "closet-praising" because I stopped worrying about being judged by other people. I am a living witness to what God can and will do when you yield to Him. In addition, I am so beyond blessed that God decided to use me as a vessel for His work. The *L.I.V.E. Commitment* helped me to embrace and to uncover the real me so that I may walk in the light of deliverance. Therefore, I will continue to stand as a victor and give God all of the glory.

Despite the challenges that you may encounter as you traverse through life, the personal value that you hold for yourself should not change. You may feel a greater sense of value in a custom-made suit, but you should also feel that you are just as valuable in an unbranded robe. If you are hiding behind some type of camouflage, you have to be willing to expose the real you so that you can be free. You need to keep in mind that you cannot experience the fullness of God as long as you are in bondage so you must liberate yourself. Throughout your journey, stay connected to God and let Him direct your path. Remember, you are to live through your challenges and not allow your challenges to live through you.

Also, you should be committed to growing in every area of your life. You have to love yourself from a front-row seat and be an all-seasons ticket holder in your own life. You have to discard your garbage and digest your goals as you press forward. You have to rely on your *divine GPS* as your primary source of guidance and triumph. When you assess your personal network, you should only seek to operate in a network that is advocating your growth. You must encourage yourself based on the unconditional interconnection that you have with God.

Even with the most difficult tribulations, you have to rest in your faith that God desires the best for you, and so should you. A faithful relationship with God will ensure that you reside in a state of contentment, and not complacency.

I Choose to L.I.V.E. was not only written for women or victims of abuse, but to try to help anyone that has been hindered by their own personal struggle. The bondage of a personal struggle can go unrealized and may cause a state of happiness that is counterfeit. The *L.I.V.E. Commitment* was not created to provide a basis for superiority, but to provide some steps on how to experience life without being bound. Now, when you make the personal commitment to:

- LOVE yourself from a front-row seat
- INVEST in yourself by internalizing your goals
- Find VICTORY in yourself with your *divine GPS*
- ENCOURAGE yourself because of God in your network

You Choose to L.I.V.E.!

L.I.V.E. SUMMARY SCRIPTURES

LOVE

"¹⁴ I will praise You, for I am fearfully *and* wonderfully made; Marvelous are Your works, and *that* my soul knows very well." (Psalm 139:14, NKJV)

"¹⁶ Therefore we do not lose heart. Even though our outward *man* is perishing, yet the inward man is being renewed day by day." (2 Corinthians 4:16, NKJV)

INVEST

"⁷ Do not be not deceived, God is not mocked; for whatever a man sows, that he will also reap." (Galatians 6:7, NKJV)

"⁵ 'I am the vine, you *are* the branches. He who abides in Me, and I in him, bears much fruit; for without Me you can do nothing.'" (John 15:5, NKJV)

VICTORY

"⁴ You are of God, little children, and have overcome them, because He who is in you is greater than he who is in the world." (1 John 4:4, NKJV)

"⁹ And He said to me, 'My grace is sufficient for you, for My strength is made perfect in weakness.' Therefore most gladly I will rather boast in my infirmities, that the power of Christ may rest upon me. ¹⁰ Therefore I take pleasure in infirmities, in reproaches, in needs, in persecutions, in distresses, for Christ's sake. For when I am weak, then I am strong." (2 Corinthians 12:9-10, NKJV)

ENCOURAGE

"²⁸ 'Come to Me, all *you* who labor and are heavy laden, and I will give you rest.'" (Matthew 11:28, NKJV)

"³¹ But those who wait on the LORD Shall renew *their* strength; They shall mount up with wings like eagles, They shall run and not be weary, They shall walk and not faint." (Isaiah 40:31, NKJV)

ABOUT THE AUTHOR

Dr. Saunya M. Williams was born in Pittsburgh, PA and spent a large amount of her childhood in San Diego, CA. With respect to her family, she was a first-generation college student and graduate. She earned a Bachelor of Science in Electrical Engineering from North Carolina A&T State University, a Master of Science in Engineering in Electrical Engineering from the University of Michigan, and a Doctor of Philosophy in Electrical and Computer Engineering from the Georgia Institute of Technology.

To overcome depression, Dr. Williams wrote inspirational notes on various scraps of paper that eventually turned into an electronic presentation that she used as spiritual therapy for herself. Later, Dr. Williams was given the opportunity to share her presentation and experiences, which became the encouragement for her to do more with her testimony. She had the desire to reach more people and wanted to tell the world about what God had done in her life. Subsequently, God gave her the task to write a book about her testimony in an effort to bring more souls to Jesus Christ and to help heal the broken.

Dr. Williams is a proud member of Elizabeth Baptist Church (EBC) led by the Senior Pastor, Dr. Craig L. Oliver, Sr. in Atlanta, GA. She is the leader of the Speechless Mime Ministry at EBC and loves to glorify God with her gift of interpretation. For several years, she had only ministered to the lyrics that gospel artists sang about, but finally decided to answer the call to tell her own story. She welcomes the opportunity to expand her ministry and to be a witness to how awesome God truly is! Today, *I Choose To L.I.V.E.* continues to be the foundation that has enabled Dr. Williams to forgive, to fulfill her purpose, and to walk without shame.

For more information, please visit: www.saunyawilliams.com.

NOTES

NOTES

NOTES

NOTES

www.ingramcontent.com/pod-product-compliance
Lightning Source LLC
Chambersburg PA
CBHW070655050426
42451CB00008B/369